Why You Need a Business Plan

Chapter:1 What Is a Business Plan?

Chapter:2 How to Choose the Right Domain Name

Chapter:3 Getting Started with Word Press

Chapter:4 The Future of Google Search Engine Rankings

Chapter:5 Using QR Codes to Make Money with Mobile Marketing

Chapter:6 Less Expensive Paid Methods

Chapter:7 Identifying the Right Software for Your Internet Marketing Business

Chapter:8 Filling Your Lists with the Right Subscribers.

Chapter:9 Email Marketing: Knowing What to Send and When.

If you are seeking to open a new business – either online or in the real world – and you don't have the capital, you will need to seek help from institutional or individual investors. And the first thing they are going to want to see before they invest a dime in your business is your business plan.

Chapter:1

What Is a Business Plan?

The business plan serves two essential functions:

It provides a blueprint that you can use to build your business

The business plan explains to investors why your business will be financially successful

What investors want to see is a business plan that presents a model of what your business will look like from its very beginning until it is operating at full capacity. Your business plan should include realistic, attainable objectives. If it includes unrealistic revenue forecasts or is built on a swampy foundation, your business plan won't fly.

Benefits of a Business Plan

Even if you are going to be your business' only employee and work out of your home, you still need a business plan. That's because your business needs a map that leads it where you want it to go.

Although your business plan should be as detailed as possible, the larger and more complicated your business will be, the more detail your business plan will need to include.

You will need to rely on your business plan and reference it frequently both before and after you launch your business, so it's absolutely necessary that you have everything in place as much as possible from the beginning.

Elements of a Business Plan

Successful business plans have five elements:

Background Information – How and why are you creating this business? Here you will include general information such as what types of products and/or services you will be selling.

Marketing Plan – Explain what type of marketing you plan to use to promote your business, such as paid advertising, social media marketing and direct marketing.

Operational Plan – Indicate how your business will function. Include hours of operation, estimated number of employees, location, and any other relevant operational data.

Financial Plan – This may be the most important part. You need to explain your financial goals and a detailed account of your estimated costs, including payroll, rent, overhead, supplies, raw materials and any other expenditure.

Decision-Making Criteria – In this section, indicate what types of things you are going to consider before moving forward with the plan.

Every business plan is different. There's not one single template you can use and simply fill in the specific details of your business proposal. When developing your plan, present the information so that anybody can use it as a tool to decide whether or not to proceed with the business.

Getting Help with Your Business Plan

If you have a partner, they ca n assist you in developing your business plan. Others who can help you include your accountant, if you have one. In most cases, CPAs have enough experience to identify glaring errors so you can correct them before showing it to anybody else.

Your next stop should be trusted professionals in the same field as yours. While you may not want to hand your business plan to somebody you will be competing against directly, if you have a friend, a former business school professor you are still close with, or a mentor who can give you genuine, helpful advice, see if they would be willing to take a look at your business plan.

When you have as much feedback as you need and have made the necessary changes to your plan so it is as accurate and realistic as possible, you can use it to attract investors. When you present to investors or apply for a business loan, your business plan will serve as the centerpiece of your pitch.

Chapter:2

How to Choose the Right Domain Name.

A domain name is the web address people click on when they want to visit your website. You need to choose your domain name before you begin building your website.

Your domain should be easy to remember, tell your customers what your website is about, be inviting, and get the customer excited about visiting your website, as well as be related to the name of your business or niche.

It's also a good idea to include keywords that help users understand what services your business provides. For example, if you own a small business called "The Baseball Card Store," choosing the domain name BaseballCardStore.com meets all five of these criteria.

Choosing the Best Domain Name

To understand how to choose the best domain name for your website, it's helpful to know a little bit about how people use the Internet. While there are billions of websites available online, people search for the ones they are interested in by using search engines like Google.com and Bing.com.

Google – the largest and most important search engine in the U.S. – uses a search engine algorithm that has digital "spiders" that crawl through the web constantly looking for new websites.

When a spider finds a new page, it scans the page and then indexes it according to the keywords that are included in its domain name, headline, content, and other places on the page.

Keywords are how the spider knows what the website is all about. The algorithm then compares that website with other websites with the same or similar keywords and ranks them all according to how useful it thinks the page will be to its users.

So when somebody types keywords into Google, the Search Engine Results Page (SERP) generates what it thinks are the most helpful websites based on those specific keywords.

Using Keywords in Your Domain Name

Putting the best keywords in your domain name will help get your page ranked in the Number 1 spot on the SERP for those keywords, or at least on the first page. Most people who land on that SERP will click on the top result. And hardly anybody ever goes further than the first page.

In general, the shorter your domain name, the easier it will be for people to remember. The maximum domain length is 64 characters, but for optimal results, you should limit your domain name to 15 characters or less. One way to do that is to use abbreviations, acronyms, and homophones that make your domain name brief, fun, interesting, and memorable.

The last three letters that come after the period are the suffix for your domain. They often provide information about what the website is about or where it originates. For example, domain names that end in .edu or .gov usually are owned by educational institutions or governments, respectively. And domain names that end in .ca or .uk originate in Canada or the United Kingdom, for example.

The Best Suffix

While you can buy domain names that end with many different suffixes, it's a good idea to choose a domain name that ends in .com, because that is the default suffix that most people – about 60% – will look for automatically. Domains that end in .net are the second-most popular (14%) while .org are third (10%).

If the purpose of your website is to promote your company's product or services or promote you or your interests, you might consider buying a domain that features your name or the name of your company. For example, ChicagoBears.com, is short, essential, and tells the website visitor what the page is all about instantly.

When most people launch a web page, they purchase a domain name, which is the name of the website that also serves as the URL, or web address, that users are directed to find it. Examples of domain names are "HowToLoseWeight.com" or "eBay.com".

These domains aren't purchased indefinitely. Instead, they are purchased only for a year or two at a time. The original buyers of these domain names typically will be given the first opportunity to renew them after the contracted time has expired. If they don't and nobody else buys them, then these domains are considered to be "expired".

The Value of Expired Domains

Even after a domain has expired, it will still get visitors. When they land on that page, they usually are directed to an error page.

Expired domains are one of the most lucrative investments on the Internet because many expired domains already have lots of backlinks already pointing to them. So in many cases, there is already a consistent flow of traffic to these domains. But because there is no actual website to take advantage of this traffic, it is wasted.

Buying Expired Domains

Some expired domains can be purchased for as little as $7 per year. After you purchase one, you can redirect it toward your affiliate link or a CPA offer so that you can receive the benefit of all this pre-created backlink traffic on autopilot.

If you are pointing the expired link you buy to an affiliate link, choose an affiliate product that is in the same niche as the expired domain so that your conversions are as high as possible.

Where to Find Expired Domains

Finding expired domains is simple. The biggest provider of expired domains is GoDaddy.com. Go to their domain auction site to search for expired domains as well as those that are about to expire. GoDaddy even tells you how much traffic they receive, as well as the current bid price.

Expired domains generally cost between $10 and $50 year for popular domains. Buy an expired domains with a lot of traffic that is similar to your affiliate product or CPA offer niche, then redirect it to your products or offer and all that monthly traffic is yours.

Getting the Most from Expired Domains

You can maximize the money you make with expired domains by identifying high value domains that are available for the lowest possible prices. When you win these auctions, relist them for auction and sell them to somebody else for more than you paid for them.

Parking Links on Expired Domains

Another option is to "park" links to your affiliate products or CPA offer on an expired domain. This is done by inserting affiliate banners for products related to the expired domain.

You can park an expired domain for as little as $1 per month and use those links to generate sales worth way more than the $12 per year you are paying for that that particular site.

Exploiting expired domains is one way to achieve online marketing success

People are often intimidated by building their own websites,

because they think you need to know a lot about writing code, graphic interfaces, and other technical issues.

That may have been the case a decade or so ago, but today, anybody can build their own website quickly and for free, once they know a few tricks of the trade.
When you use the free tools and theme templates available at open-source sites like WordPress, building a high-quality website is easy.

"Open source" means that anybody can use it and you don't have to pay to use its tools. WordPress is very easy to use and even has hundreds of free tutorial videos you can watch that show you how to do every step.

WordPress has thousands of premade "themes," which are website templates that you can use for free starting right away. It also offers paid themes.

Another benefit of WordPress is that it has a lot of free plug-ins that you can drag and drop onto your website, including such things as creating automated links to your Facebook, Twitter, and other social media pages, polls, and other desirable additions to your web pages.

Plus, WordPress makes it super easy to add photos, images, video, and audio recordings to your website. And you don't even need to know anything about HTML or CSS code writing. If you can drag and drop, you have all the skills you need to create a high-quality, professional-looking website.

Chapter:3

Getting Started with Word Press.

The first thing you need to do is create an account with WordPress. It's free and only takes a few minutes. All you really need is an email address, and you are ready to go.

Go to the WordPress home page and click on the "Get Started" button. Here you can set up your free account and choose a name for your website. You will be sent an email with a link that activates your WordPress account. Now you are ready to build your page.

Whenever you log into WordPress, you will automatically be brought to your Dashboard. This is the place where you create new web pages, choose themes, add new features, and do everything else you need to build and maintain your website pages.

On the left-hand side of your Dashboard, there are a set of buttons you use to create your settings, make changes, and add new elements to your website. The first couple of times you use WordPress, you're going to want to take the time to learn about these tools by watching the free tutorial videos that explain how to use them.

3 Steps to Creating High-Converting Headlines

Headlines are the single most important part of any marketing document, be it an email, a sales letter, squeeze page or paid advertisement. That's because the headline is your first and only opportunity to capture the attention of the prospective customer.

If you headline fails to make an instant, immediate impression upon your reader, they will stop reading further and probably are lost to you forever.

The best headlines – those that grasp your page visitor by the lapels, shake them up and refuse to let go – share three common traits. If you ensure that your headlines always includes these three qualities, you can attract a greater number of prospects to spend more time with your copy and enhance your chances of converting them into a long-term customer, which is the ultimate objective of any marketing document.

Clarity Is King

The first and most important quality of any great headline is that it can be immediately understood by anybody who is reading it. The more clarity a headline has, the more appealing it will be to page visitors.

If your headline is in any way ambiguous, confusing, or doesn't provide a clear and concise message that can be grasped instantly, it is going to turn readers away in droves. Clear, easy to understand headlines should be as specific as possible.

Remember, the people who are landing on your pages or seeing your ads are looking for solutions and answers. The last thing they want to do is to spend more time trying to figure out what is meant by an ambiguous or uncertain headline. Be as clear as you can possibly be.

Headlines Have Two Parts

The most effective headlines have two parts: The headline itself and the sub-headline, also known as the "sub-head". One way to think of it is like this: The headline is the bait that gets the prospect in the door and the sub-head is what you use to hook them in so they will keep reading.

A clear and concise headline is critical, but by itself it usually is not enough to fully engage the reader. It needs help – in the form of a great, informative sub-head that boosts the clarity the reader gets from the headline.

The sub-head acts to reaffirm the reason why your reader has landed on your page or looked at your ad in the first place. It should set the stage for the story your content is about to tell them.

The Best Headlines Include Numbers

There is a whole body of research that proves that people using the Internet are astronomically more likely to click through on a headline that includes a number than one that simply includes words. This has something to do with the way our minds are wired.

Numbers express certainty. They subconsciously tell the reader that there message expressed in the headline is based on substance and fact, so people seeking solutions or answers online are naturally more attracted to headlines that include numbers than they are to just words.

The numbers you put in your headlines can include all kinds of figures, including percentages, the amount of things on lists, time measurements, and so on:

"3-Day Free Trial for All New Subscribers"
"Top 5 Ways to Shed Weight Fast"
"Increase Sales by 30% in 30 Days Using This One Weird Trick"

Generally, the number will be in the main headline rather than the sub-head. But the information in the sub-head should support whatever number you include in the headline.
These three qualities are so widely used that headlines that don't include them are often perceived as jarring or off-putting – and usually fail to convert. Successful marketers understand what works and what doesn't, so they gravitate toward the tried and true in order to maximize their results.

If you keep your headlines clear and to the point, include sub-headlines that support the primary point of the main headline, and include numbers to give your headline substance and authority, you can exponentially increase your conversion rates regardless of what type of marketing document you are using.

Creating Your First Web Page

To build your first new web page on WordPress, click on the "Posts" button on your Dashboard, and then click on "Add New." This automatically generates a new page.

There's a space for the headline or title and a box underneath for your content. You will also find different icons that perform various functions, including using different typefaces, bullet points, adding links, and adding images and other media.

WordPress will automatically save drafts as you build your web page. Or you can click on the "Save Draft" button. To see what your page will look like to visitors, click on the "Preview" button at any time. When you are happy with the final version of your web page, click on the "Publish" button, and your web page will instantly be posted to your server.

You can edit or modify your web page anytime you want, even after you have posted it online. Changes are automatically updated, so anybody who goes to your page will only see the latest version. You also can delete portions of your website, or even the entire web page itself, any time you want.

Land Your Web Page in the Three Top Spots in Google Results

Getting ranked on Google's search engine results pages (SERPs) is a zero sum game. If you can capture one of three top spots, or at least Page 1, your website is practically guaranteed to get a lot of visitors. If you are on any other page, most potential customers will never find you. Effects of Google's Algorithm Updates Just when most web masters got search engine optimization (SEO) figured out, Google changed the way it ranked pages. In August 2011, it launched its Panda search engine algorithm update.

 The biggest difference was that Google starting putting much less emphasis on backlinks and gave more weight to social approval signals. This shift continued when the Penguin update was rolled out in April 2012. Google's search engine algorithm originally was designed before the explosion in popularity of social media. In these seemingly pre-historic days – which actually were less than a decade ago – web users had few opportunities to respond immediately to the content they were reading.

 As a result, a website's ranking was based primarily on how many high-quality backlinks it had. Social Approval Signals Penguin and Panda changed all that. Now a site's ranking is mainly determined by Internet users who can "vote" on the usefulness and quality of a site by hitting the Facebook "Like" button, re-Tweeting it, using the "+1" button on Google Plus.

 Google uses these social approval signals to determine a web page's value faster and more accurately. As a result, its search engine algorithm relies more heavily on social media-based indicators, rather than backlinks, to determine a site's page ranking. So if you want your page ranked high, you need to make it easy for people to give it social approval signals. Search engine marketing (SEM) needs to focus on encouraging people on social media to link to and approve their pages, rather than focusing most of their time creating backlinks, which are still useful but no longer of primary importance.

 Using LSI Keywords While including the optimal number of keywords related to your niche – 2 to 4 percent — is still critically important to improving your Google ranking, the Penguin version is now also looking for Latent Semantic Indexing Keywords (LSIs), a fancy term that basically means "synonyms." Google now gives preference to web pages that flow more organically, so pages that are optimally saturated with synonyms for the keyword are preferred to those stuffed with the same keyword stated over and over again.

 Page Visitor Behavior Another critical change is the value Google's search engine now pays attention to the behavior of your page's visitors once they arrive there. In addition to looking at things like how long the average visitor stays on your page and how frequently they return, the post-Penguin search engine also considers such things as your click-through, surf pattern and bounce rate – or how many visitors click away from your page after only a second or two, an indicator of a sub-quality page.

 If visitors don't find what they are looking for when they arrive on your site, find your content to be dull, uninteresting, or consider your content to be the same they can find everywhere else, your bounce rate will increase. Another thing that can increase bounce rate is when pages have audio or video that starts automatically. This tends to cause visitors to bounce off right away, especially if they are viewing the page at work.   Decreasing 'Bounce Rate' To reduce your bounce rate, you want to make it easier for high-target visitors to find your page and provide high-value content once they arrive there. These SEM techniques will keep your visitors engaged longer improving the way Google ranks your page. Another thing to consider is the keywords that are attracting your page's visitors:

 Are they the most appropriate? If not, users who arrive and don't find what they want are likely to leave quickly, negatively affecting your SERP rank. Finally, design your page by including clearly-defined links within it to other pages within your site so that visitors can easily navigate to the specific information they want. This helps to reduce page bounce and to keep visitors on your pages longer, both of which improve ranking. If you'd like to learn more about making money online, as well as a way to generate conversion-ready Internet marketing prospects each month,

3 Ways to Build Trust with Your Page Visitors

The fastest and most effective way to engage your readers into your content is to draw them into a story. People are naturally pre-disposed to want and enjoy stories. If you can wrap your web page content in an engaging story that connects emotionally with your reader, you have a better chance of getting them to follow your call to action.

The Power of Your Personality

The story you create can be either your own first person account of something that changed your life, or it can be the story of somebody else, such as a character you create. In either case, the purpose of the story is to get the reader to connect with the subject of the story. The problems or challenges you or your character experience should be the same problems your readers are having.

The story you create naturally needs to have a happy ending. In the case of sales copy, for example, it will always be the way the product solved the problem and improved the subject's life forever.

When your prospective customer relates with the story's subject, they project the solution your product is creating onto their own problems, making them more open to the idea of purchasing your product.

Whether you use a character-driven or first-person narrative, it's important that you inject your personality into the story. Try to use familiar language that makes it easier for the reader to make a connection with the story you are telling them. This will put them at ease and help them see more clearly the benefits of your product in their lives.

Creating Trust in the Product's Power

The character you feature in your story may be the nominal subject, but the true hero needs to be whatever you are promoting in your call to action.

For example, if you are creating a sales page for an eBook on how to cure acne, your story will describe the horrible problems that acne created in your life or that of your character.

But the true hero of the story will be the product that you discovered that cured your acne forever and caused radical improvements to your life: You gained more confidence, you were more popular than ever, your sex appeal increased and you finally found true happiness, for example.

Social Proof

Web copy frequently uses social proof to reinforce the positive message about the product they are promoting. Social proof is sometimes referred to as the "bandwagon approach" because it feeds the natural human psychological desire to be part of a larger group.

Your web page visitors will be more open to following your call to action if they believe others already use and endorse your product. According to Google, 70% of Americans now say they look at product reviews before making a purchase. Adding testimonials to your sales page is often enough to tip your readers into making a buying decision.

How to Get Testimonials

Obtaining testimonials isn't as daunting a task as most people believe. In fact, it's actually quite easy.

First, it should be noted that you don't want to make up testimonials. That would be dishonest and also a violation of Federal Trade Commission regulations.

But there is nothing preventing you legally or ethically from asking family members or friends to write testimonials for you. You are not required to disclose your relationship with the person who gives you a product testimonial.

Another option is to send emails to people who already have purchased your product and ask if they would be willing to write a brief testimonial. In most cases, if you ask for somebody's help they will happily give it to you. This is especially true if your customers are already satisfied with the quality of your product.

Seeking Endorsements

A third option is to offer your product for free to people who are considered to be authoritative in your niche.

For example, if the original product you created is a video series on how to improve your golf swing, you could reach out to club pros in your city. Send them your product for free with the request that if they found it helpful to send you a brief testimonial that you could include with future marketing collateral.

Even if only a couple respond, you can use their testimonials in marketing materials for many years to come.

Fast and Easy Ways to Build Your Social Media Influence

Google's updated search engine algorithm assigns more value to websites that receive a lot of social approval signals. These are indications that social media users find these pages useful or helpful and include such things as Facebook "Likes", how many times a link to the page has been posted on Twitter, and the number of "+1's" a site has on Google+.

To increase these social approval signals on your web pages, you need to be active on social media. The bigger the number of your social media contacts, the more opportunities you have to get social approval signals for your web pages to improve their Google rankings.

Increasing Your Social Approval Signals

Once you have a lot of social media contacts, you need to post frequently on social media. Don't always blast your social network with commercial offerings or they will ignore your future postings or ban you altogether.

Instead, alternate your commercial postings with a wealth of free high-quality content. Forward links and postings that you found interesting, and try to create a personal link with your network members by posting lots of personal information, pictures and non-controversial comments.

Get social with your visitors as well. When they leave comments, make sure to respond to them quickly.

Try to establish yourself as an expert by providing valuable, accurate information that your network can actually use. This will increase the likelihood that they pass it along to their networks and also can improve your authorship weight by convincing Google that you are an authoritative content provider.

Social Signal Velocity

Google's search engine doesn't just measure how many social signals your web page receives. It also looks at how quickly people respond to them. This is known as the social signal velocity.

If you add a posting to your web page and 10 people "Like" it or give it a "+1" over the course of the next month, that has far less value to Google's search engine than if 10 people "voted" for it within the first hour of its posting. Google now measures the immediate impact of a website's posting as well as its long-term value to users.

Other Ways to Build Your Social Influence

In addition to building your influence on social media, there are other things you can do to dramatically improve your chances of staying on top of the Google rankings.

The first is blogging. If you don't already have a blog, you should create one. Blogging is quickly becoming the most common way for like-minded people to share ideas and information with each other online.

Blogs are free to set up and distribute. And existing blogging networks, such as WordPress and Blogger, already include free tools that make it easy to connect with people who are passionately interested in your product niche. Creating frequent, original, highly-informative blogs that include links to your web pages also is an effective and cost-free way of building your audience and cross-promoting your business.

Exploiting the Rising Popularity of Video

The second way to build your online profile is videos. As playback technology becomes universal, more Internet users are migrating from text-based sites to video, which is faster and easier to absorb.

Converting your content to video is relatively easy using the video recording equipment now included in almost every electronic device, including smartphones, laptops and tablets.

The most popular videos are those that explain how to do something, so if there is a way for you to present helpful information to your social network using videos, you should use it. Just don't forget to include links to your web pages and to optimize your videos with the most effective keywords.

Finally, whatever type of content you create always be consistent with tone, style, design, colors and logos. These are all elements of creating your brand.

You can strengthen the effectiveness of your social signal campaigns by creating an effective, recognizable brand in the minds of your social network. The more you do to build the comfort level of your visitors, the more likely they will be to want to spread the word about your content to their own network of friends and family.

Chapter:4

The Future of Google Search Engine Rankings.

Because everyone is now plugged into the Internet, the way people communicate with each other is faster than ever.

Texting is immediate. Using a social signal to indicate preference is quicker than word of mouth. This type of instant approval has had a profound impact on online marketing. It has killed backlink marketing and put email marketing on life support.

Today's Internet users – especially younger users – process shorter burst of information more quickly and tend to have much shorter attention spans. As technology improves and speeds get even faster, this trend will only continue in the future.

Backlink Overkill

While backlinks are still helpful in building your sites rankings – especially when they come from authoritative or expert sites – they are aren't nearly as important as they once were. A decade ago, the number of backlinks a site had was the primary measure of its relevance to Google search engines.

But unethical web users effectively ruined this for everybody by creating commercial and black-hat SEO methods that artificially increased the number of backlinks a particular site had. Google's Panda and Penguin updates to its search engine algorithm at the beginning of this decade were designed to counteract these inorganic SEO techniques.

Social Approval Signals

After backlinks essentially became corrupted, Google's search engine development team turned to social approval signals as a more natural, organic way of measuring a web page's popularity.

While there are still plenty of black hat methods people use to artificially inflate the amount of social signals a site receives – such as creating fake Facebook pages or purchasing "Likes" or "+1s" on Fiverr.com – Google's search engine is better equipped to detect bot-produced Tweets and other phony social media recommendations.

It also gives more weight to social signals from those social media users who are the most active and who have the largest social networks.

A website's page ranking now depends on its ability to get visitors to "vote" for the site by promoting it on their social media pages or to their social media contacts. As a result, it's critical that web page owners make it as easy as possible for page visitors to share pages or give social approval signals.

You should always include buttons on your pages that allow visitors to instantly link them to their

Facebook, Twitter, LinkedIn and Google Plus accounts, as well as to social bookmarking sites such as Digg, Pinterest and StumbleUpon.

If you use WordPress or another popular page-creation site, you can use free drag-and-drop plug-ins to include these buttons on your website. Make sure you display them prominently near the top of the page so that visitors can click on them faster and more easily because not all visitors will scroll all the way to the bottom of your web page.

Google +

Recognizing how improvements to internet access have increased the importance of social media, Google is taking aim at Facebook and Twitter and is positioning Google Plus to be the premier social media site in the years to come.

Google+ has more applications to businesses as well as to individuals than most other social media platforms. It's "Circles" method of grouping contacts lends itself easily to marketing toward specific groups of customers. And Google's purchase of YouTube, the world's most popular video sharing site, makes the company the web's top provider of video, the fastest-growing content delivery format in the world.

While Facebook and Twitter continue to be important, your social media marketing programs in the coming years need to include Google+ because it is poised to be the most important social media site in the future.

Google has slowly and carefully rolled out its newest features and has yet to devote its full considerable resources to properly marketing the service. But Google+ has all the tools it needs to become the premier social media site on the internet.

6 Ways to Monetize Your website

If you have a successful website with a lot of subscribers who look forward to your high quality content – or if your website is shared frequently via social media – then making money with your website is a relatively simple process.

Here are some fast and easy ways to make money with your existing website:

#1: Promote Affiliate Products

Within your blog's content, you can reference affiliate products that you promote. These can be promoted either within the content itself, or as the focal point of the blog posting, such as product review or an endorsement.

#2: Click-Per-Action Offers

Click-Per-Action, or CPA, is when you get paid by a third party when visitors to your blog or website take a particular action, such as giving you their email address. There are many CPA networks you can go to find CPA offers you can include in our blog.

Some CPA networks offer payouts of just a few cents for every blog reader you get to click through to the offer while others can pay several dollars per click-through. The offers can be related directly to the content of your blog or entirely unrelated.

#3: Brand Placement

When you promote a particular brand or product within your blog, this is known as brand placement. If you have a lot of loyal subscribers, have a reputation as an expert in your field, or have a very popular that is frequently cited in the media, many advertisers will pay to be associated with your blog.

Usually, companies will approach the blogs or websites they want to place their brand or products in. But nothing prevents you from approaching companies and offering to promote their brands within our blog's content, especially if your blog is already popular.

#4: Add a Mailing List/Newsletter Opt-In Form

Add a mailing list/newsletter opt-in form to your blog. When people sign up, use the subscriber list to promote products and services or sell the list to other bloggers or Internet marketers.

Every online business wants access to large, highly targeted email lists. When you have the addresses of people who proven to be interested in your niche, all you need to do is use your autoresponder to manage an email marketing campaign to promote your own products or services or those of other marketers.

#5: Sell Display Advertising

If your blog is self-hosted, you can sell as much display advertising you want and keep all the profits for yourself. What you can charge for ads depends on how many regular subscribers you have and on your reputation as a blogger

Ads can be placed the ads at the top, in the margins, or at the bottom of your blog page. You can charge advertisers per impression – in other words, a set amount per 1,000 viewers of your blog — or you can charge a fixed rate for an entire month.

#6: In-Text Advertising

Another type of ad you can sell on a self-hosted blog is in-text advertising. Links are placed inside your text and come with a double underline to differentiate them from normal links. When a user rolls the mouse over the link, a pop-up ad will appear that leads viewers to your advertiser's web page or offer.

Writing blogs to share your specialized knowledge with other people is fun and rewarding. But there's no reason you shouldn't make money at the same time, especially given all the hard work and effort that goes into producing, promoting and distributing a high-quality, informative blog.

Chapter:5

Using QR Codes to Make Money with Mobile Marketing.

Quick Response Codes, or QR Codes for short, are those funny looking little black and white squibs that you see on subway signs, magazine advertisements and lots of other places these days.

QR Codes are a variation of the bar code – also known as the Universal Product Code (UPC) – which has been used since the 1970s at retail checkout areas. Bar codes also are commonly used for inventory purposes.

QR Codes were first used in 1994, when engineers at a Japanese factory owned by a subsidiary of Toyota wanted to create a three-dimensional version of the bar code that could hold exponentially more information and that could be decoded at faster speeds. The first QR Code was used to control the inventory of automobile parts as they moved through the manufacturing process.

How QR Codes Work

Unlike UPCs – which are mechanically scanned by a narrow beam of light – QR Codes are scanned as a two-dimensional image by a semiconductor image sensor. This image is then digitally analyzed by the processor the scanning device.

The processor detects the three distinctive squares at the corners of the image, and – with the help of a fourth smaller square in the fourth corner – automatically converts the image into a standard size, orientation and angle of viewing. The tiny dots are then converted into binary code, which is matched against an error-detecting code.

The binary code can represent anything, such as text or an image, but in most cases it is a Uniform Resource Locator (URL), or an Internet address.

Uses and Benefits

Anybody with a mobile phone or tablet can scan a QR Code. Scanning apps are free and can be downloaded instantly on iTunes, Google Apps, the Android store and elsewhere.

Other apps let users generate and print their own QR Codes for others to scan and be diverted a device to a URL, eliminating the need to the user to copy down and type in a web address.

QR Codes are used widely in advertising. But they also can be used by online marketers to promote offers and to send traffic to web pages. Other uses for QR Codes include:

Visiting a Google+ or Facebook profile

Showing your branding on textiles such as t-shirts or bags and other articles like mugs

Checking in on recommendation services like foursquare

Using QR codes in blogs

Playing a YouTube video

Easily installing an app from the App Store or Android Market

Sending a predefined short message (premium services)

Sending a Tweet with your content

Mobile Marketing Uses

QR Codes are most frequently used for mobile marketing. They are supported by Google's mobile Android operating system; in iOS devices such as the iPhone, iPad and iPod; on BlackBerry devices, on the Windows Phone, and even on the Nintendo 3DS.

Once scanned, QR Codes can use a URL to lead users to website where they can view useful content. This can include expanded product information, locations and store hours of the places where the product can be purchased, and even links to buy the product right away.

QR Codes also can be used for mobile tagging. This is when you capture the reading device's phone number and automatically send an email or text message either right away or at some predetermined future time. Mobile tagging also can launch a sequence of email swipes designed to build excitement and encourage brand loyalty.

Traffic Optimization Secrets Most People Don't Know About

When it comes down to it, making money with Internet marketing isn't rocket science. All you have to do is use paid or free methods that lead visitor to your offers, then utilize techniques within our content that maximize conversion rates.

Without a doubt, paying for traffic is the easiest way to build your online business. You can sometimes get results within a few hours – or even a few minutes – of launching your paid traffic campaigns. But as soon as the money runs out, usually so does the traffic.

The paid platform most marketers use is Google AdWords. It's the biggest and most popular. But therein lies the problem: Google AdWords is so big that it's often really hard to get your offers noticed by consumers. It's simply so filled with competitors that you either have to spend a fortune bidding on the best keywords or risk getting little return for your marketing dollar.

Plus, Google has one of the worst support structures you are going to find anywhere. It also has built a reputation for being hostile toward affiliate marketers. Google has been known to ban accounts suddenly and without explanation. And they are so big, they can get away with it!

Alternatives to Google AdWords

But Google isn't the only game in town. For many marketers, Bing and Yahoo offer better alternatives.

While between the two, Bing and Yahoo only account for 29.2% of the search engine marketplace, that's 29% of billions of online users. And both are not only affiliate friendly, but provide better service.

Best of all, while your competitors are spending a fortune bidding on the best keywords on Google, you can quietly but effectively promote your offers on Bing and Yahoo without overspending on the best keywords.

Chapter: 6

Less Expensive Paid Methods

Two other little-used but highly effective paid methods are Facebook Ads and solo ads.

Even though Facebook seems to share Google's contempt for affiliate marketers, its ad program is worth considering because of its ability to provide extremely targeted demographic and psychographic information so you can tailor your offers not only on things like age, gender and geographic location, but also on likes and dislikes, interests and preferences.

The biggest benefit of solo ads is the price. Your budget go much farther using solo ads as compared to working with a bigger, more expensive marketing platform. And your ads are seen only by people who already have proven to be passionate about your niche.

Secret Free Traffic Methods

Right now, social approval signals are the top measure of site ranking. But creating back links to your web pages from high authority sites still can influence your page's rankings.

Search engines consider authority sites to be anyplace web users go when they are searching for answers to niche-related questions. They include such site as Wikipedia.com, About.com, eHow.com, Yahoo Answers, and so on. Sites with the suffix .gov and .edu also are considered authority sites by the search engines.

Creating Links from Authoritative Sites

Here's a fast, easy way to create links to your pages from authoritative sites:

Go to any of these sites

Create an article or comment on an existing post

Leave a link to your pages in the About the Author box

When readers follow that link back to your page, you have a new high-target prospect and your page ranking will improve at the same time.

When you use these traffic generating secrets, you don't have to spend a fortune promoting your offers or attracting new visitors to your web pages.

Chapter: 7

Identifying the Right Software for Your Internet Marketing Business

Using software programs can be an effective way to make your online promotions work more efficiently and profitably for you. For example, some software programs can mine a large amount of data in order to give you only the information that will be helpful to you, such as customer lists sorted according to geographic areas or preferences.

How Much Should You Spend?

Software that can help your internet marketing business be more successful usually requires the purchase of software and/or licensing fees. Others like subscriber lists or sales leads may be pay-per-use, but most charge both a set-up and a monthly use fee.

While it may seem like a lot to have to pay both a set-up fee and a subscription fee, this often actually is to your advantage because technology changes very rapidly on the Internet. As a result, there are usually many different versions and upgrades of the same software available.

Paying the start-up fee and the monthly subscription usually allows you to get updated versions of the same software as they come out at no additional cost. That, in turn, lets you to keep using the same software program seamlessly.

Taking It for a Test Drive

Before you pay for software, ask if there's a free trial version you can use. If not, at least spend some time playing around with the free tools so you can see if it's going to be practical for you.

If a software seller won't let you take their product for a test drive, you may want to keep looking. And don't be fooled if they offer you a 30-day money back guarantee because it may turn out to be hard to collect your refund.

Finding the Best Software

Ask your friends or business contacts what software they use and if they like it. Usually, people are more than willing to share their experiences with you, which can save you a lot of time and money by skipping trial and error process of identifying effective software.

Don't Rely Too Heavily on Software Products

The software products you buy should make your business run more efficiently. But they aren't going to run your business for you. Don't assume that software will build your business. Only you can build your business. Software tools can only help you achieve this goal.

Yet software can be effective in helping you organize your day, manage data, and speed up some processes of marketing.

Identifying the Most Popular Software

Sometimes the best way of choosing software is to let the market guide you to the best products.

Software that has been popular over time probably is better and more functional than software that is at the top of the Android app store charts today and gone tomorrow. Market forces are generally a good guide in the long run. Software that has applications that are actually useful and help improve businesses organize their operations will always have a longer life.

What Software Should Do

When considering software, look for products that help you focus on these primary aspects of your online marketing business:

Expand your business's profile on social media platforms

Generates new leads

Improves public relations

Provides web analytics

Optimizes web design

Improve inbound marketing

Facilitate social media integration

Improve SEO for site content

When creating your web-based business, you want to ensure that it is built on the most solid foundation you can create. Software tools are often some of your first and most important investments. It pays in the long run to take the time to choose the right software options.

Chapter:8

Filling Your Lists with the Right Subscribers.

Building a big list of subscribers is a lot of work. Whether you use paid or free methods to build your lists, it's important that you fill your lists only with highly-targeted people who are passionate about your niche and are ready, willing and able to pay for the products you are promoting.

Here are some effective techniques you can use to make sure your lists are comprised only of the best possible customers who will continue to act on your offers for weeks or even years to come.

Kicking Out the Freeloaders

There are a lot of people online who are only looking to get stuff for free. These freeloaders are never going to spend money no matter what you do. Usually, they aren't hurting anybody and can be safely ignored or at least tolerated.

But why should you have to spend time and energy marketing toward them?

A better plan is to keep track of who your customers are and how much they are spending on your offers. Cater toward your best customers and drop the freeloaders.

Identify Your Best Customers

You definitely want to take care of your best customers by giving them the best deals. You also want to give them exclusive access to new products before they are offered to anyone else. Plus, you want to push them further and further up the profit ladder so that they spend increasing amounts of money with you.

If your tracking shows you subscribers aren't spending anything, it's perfectly acceptable to delete them from your list and let them go bother some other marketer.

If you want, you can send them one final email that says something like, "I noticed that you haven't purchased any of my products and I wanted to know if there was something in particular that you wanted and aren't getting from me or if there was some other reason." Sometimes this lets you convert freeloaders into loyal customers. But most of the time, this will scare them off end their trying to get free stuff from you

Benefit of Repeat Buyers

Long-term relationships with your customers are always more profitable than short-term revenues. Building long-term relationships with your customers is the most rewarding strategy for your revenues, your personal reputation, your company and your brand.

Treat customers as if they are your friends, rather than simply people who buy your products. That way you can improve the effectiveness of any marketing program. Share details about your personal history and family life. Customers that develop a genuine emotional bond with you will have a vested interest in your success.

How to Develop Long-Term Relationships with Your Customers

Nurture a personal relationship with your customers to create a unique benefit of doing business on the web. When people believe that you consider them nothing more than a customer, they will think of you as nothing more than a marketer and soon they will stop paying attention to what you have to say.

But two-way communication can overcome this hurdle. Use your marketing campaign to facilitate two-way communications so that it's easy for your customers to interact with you. For example, you can include the tag line "Let Me Know What You Think" with each posting that includes an automatic link back to your own email account or web page. That let you solicit your customer's thoughts and opinions, reinforcing their importance to you and the success of your business.

Also, whenever a customer takes the time to contact you, always send a follow-up thank you and acknowledge how important and helpful their comment was to you. This will strengthen their loyalty bond with you and your brand and make them more open to doing business with you in the future.

Chapter:9

Email Marketing: Knowing What to Send and When.

If you already have a list of subscribers who are passionate about your niche, it's time to set up a series of emails that you program your autoresponder to send out according to a pre-set schedule. This is known as an "email swipe".

There's no limit to the number of emails you can send out. Your subscribers keep getting them until they unsubscribe from your list. As long as your emails provide something your customers want, they will continue to keep opening them.

And, as long as they are opening your emails, rather than deleting theme without reading them, you have the opportunity to sell the products you are promoting to the people on your email list.

What Emails Should Do

The emails you send out should serve one of two purposes:

Reinforce your subscriber's loyalty by giving them something of high value for free

Promote a particular product or service

Effective email swipes contain both types of emails. If you send out emails that just promote products and services, your subscribers aren't going to get a lot of value from your emails and they will be more likely to unsubscribe.

Instead, alternate these promotional emails with ones that provide free high-value content that they can actually use in their everyday lives. Your subscribers then will be more likely to open your emails and to purchasing the products or services you promote when you send promotional emails.

Toggling between these two types of emails successfully requires a lot of skill, much of which comes with experience.

Keep in mind that once the person on your email list makes the choice to delete your email without reading it the first time, it's going to be harder and harder for you to get them to open any subsequent emails that you send.

That's why it is critically important that you keep your emails interesting enough and provide enough value so that the people on your list will have no choice but to open your emails every time you send them.

What Kind of Content to Include

Free high-value emails should contain either original content that you have created yourself or content you have purchased or commissioned from freelancers, PLR or some other source. Your emails can even simply contain links to informative content your subscribers will find useful.

By the way, this strategy works the same when marketing in other platforms as well, not just email. You can provide high value content and keep people looking forward to your next submission on places such as Facebook, Twitter, Instagram, Tumblr and many other formats. The principle is the same.

Consider your emails swipes as a newsletter that you send your subscribers. A newsletter contains interesting and helpful articles about topics that interesting. If your content is high quality and your subscribers enjoy it, they are going to be more open to buying the products and services you promote in your newsletter.

How Often Should You Send Emails?

While there is no agreed-upon schedule for free content and promotional emails, use a 3:1 proportion. For every promotional email you send out, send out three that provide free high value content designed to build loyalty with your subscribers.

Promotional emails should have a structure similar to a sales letter. Have a clear Call to Action (CTA) that says exactly you want your reader to do: Buy a product, subscribe to a newsletter, invest in your company, etc.

Promotional emails need to have a link where your subscribers can click on to buy the products or services you are promoting.

Content of Promotional Emails

The content you promote in your promotional emails can be either original or something you commissioned another person to create for you. You also can promote affiliate products, which are products sold by somebody else but promoted by you. When a subscriber clicks through and buys one of these affiliate products, you get paid a commission.

Affiliate products are popular among email marketers because they don't require you to purchase anything up front or worry about delivering the product to the buyer. All you do is promote the product and when a sale is made, you get paid

Follow This Email Marketing Etiquette to Get Your Delivered and Read

Email marketing can be a very effective way of bringing new customers into your sales funnel. But due to the widespread use of viruses and malware, most people are cautious about opening an email that comes from a source they don't recognize, that is strangely written, or appears to have come from a non-English speaker.

You can reassure your prospective customers that the emails you send are safe and reliable by following a few simple email marketing etiquette rules:

1. Don't Sensationalize the Headline

The default setting for Yahoo, AOL, Gmail, and the other popular email providers is to show who the sender is and the headline. In some instances, the first few words of the email text itself will appear on the user's email queue.

That makes the headline the first important element of your email. If it is overly exaggerated, makes extraordinary claims, or is otherwise sensational, there's a better chance that the email will either be sent directly to the "Spam" folder or deleted by the user without being read.

The objective is to get the reader to open the email, so your headline has to give them a reason to do so. You want to capture their imagination and engage their interest, but not go over the top. Avoid using exclamation points – especially multiple exclamation points – as well as ALL CAPS and crazy colors because this will most likely tag your email as spam.

2. Use the Person's Name, If Known

The greeting is the first thing the reader will see when they open your email. If you know the user's name (because you either know them personally, they are already on your list, or their name was included on an email list you have purchased) use your autoresponder to insert their first name in the greeting, such as "Dear Paul" or "Dear Sandra."

Email tends to be less formal than traditional letter-writing, so in most cases using the person's first name is perfectly acceptable. Using the person's last name can often seem off-putting, such as "Dear Mr. Stewart" or "Dear Ms. Simpson." Exceptions would include formal titles such as "Doctor," "Professor," or a military title.

3. Get to the Point

Because emails are less formalized than traditional letter-writing, and because people get so many emails every day, the person receiving your email probably isn't going to give it much attention. That's why it is critically important that you get to the point of your email right away, starting with the very first sentence.

In email writing, you have to give the reader a reason to keep reading. Don't waste time by beating around the bush or trying to build up to your point slowly. You have only a few moments to maintain the reader's attention, so make the most of it.

4. Signing Off

Another difference between traditional letter writing and emails is the sign-off. You don't have to include a formal "Sincerely" or "Gratefully yours."

Simply ending with your name is perfectly acceptable. Or, if you prefer, you can use an informal phrase such as "Chat with you soon" or "Cheers."

Following these general email etiquette protocols will increase the chances that the person receiving your email will open it and read it. Make sure the content of your email pushes the person to the action that you want them to perform, such as clicking on a link included in the body of your email.

www.ingramcontent.com/pod-product-compliance
Lightning Source LLC
Chambersburg PA
CBHW041950240526
45473CB00036B/2866